Ayudar a Nuestros Amigos Animales!

Dr. Robert H. Stauffer Jr.

Published by Robert Stauffer, 2024.

AYUDAR A NUESTROS AMIGOS ANIMALES!

First edition. November 5, 2024.

ISBN: 979-8230774198

Written by Dr. Robert H. Stauffer Jr..

Introduction: A Fun Adventure to Help Our Animal Friends!

Welcome to a magical world full of amazing animals! In this book, we're going to meet some very special friends—endangered animals! These animals, like the gentle manatee and the strong tiger, are super important for our planet. But right now, they need our help to stay safe and happy!

You'll go on a fun journey around the world to learn all about these awesome animals. We'll discover where they live, what they like to do, and why they need our help. Get ready for cool facts, sweet stories, and lots of ways you can be a hero for them!

Each chapter will tell you about a different endangered animal, like the big, friendly manatee that swims in the sea! You'll find out how these slow swimmers munch on yummy seagrass and what happens when their homes get dirty. We'll also learn about things like pollution and how we can help keep our animal friends safe and healthy.

As you read, remember that even small things you do can help! Telling your friends about these animals, helping groups that protect them, or taking care of our Earth are all great ways to make a difference!

So, let's jump into the exciting stories of these special animals and be their heroes! Together, we can make sure they stay safe and happy on our planet for a long, long time. Are you ready for the adventure? Let's go!

The Buzz About Bees: Why We Need to Save Our Fuzzy Friends

Hey there! Have you ever seen a bee? Those little buzzing bugs flying around flowers? Well, guess what? Bees are super important for our world, and they do way more than just make honey! They help plants grow, and without them, we could have big problems!

Why Bees Are Special

Did you know that bees help about 85% of all flowers grow? That's almost all of them! They go to flowers to collect yummy nectar, and while they're there, they help flowers make fruits and veggies. Imagine going to the store and finding no food at all! That could happen if there were no bees!

A really smart man named Albert Einstein once said, "If the bee disappears from the earth, people would have no more than four years to live." Yikes! That's scary! It's because, without bees, we wouldn't have enough food to eat.

The Honey Dance

Bees are busy little workers! They make honey and save it for winter. But guess how they find food? They do a little dance! It's true! When a bee finds the best flowers, it dances to tell its friends where to go. To make just one pound of honey, bees have to visit between 2 and 4 million flowers! That's a lot of flying and dancing!

While they're doing all that, they're also helping our fruits and veggies grow by carrying pollen from flower to flower. Without bees, yummy things like apples, strawberries, and even carrots would be much harder to find.

Are Bees in Trouble?

Right now, bees are in big trouble! Their numbers are going down because of something called pesticides. These are chemicals people spray on plants to keep bad bugs away, but sometimes they hurt bees too. One kind of pesticide, called neonicotinic pesticides, is especially harmful. Since 2004, the honeybee population has dropped by half!

If bees keep disappearing, we could run out of food. We need bees, and they need our help!

How Can We Help Bees?

The good news is there are many ways we can help save the bees:

- If you live in a backyard, you can put a bee hive in your yard to give them a safe home.

- If you have a small garden, you can plant flowers that bees love, like lavender!

- Before using any bug spray, check if it's safe for bees. You can look it up online!

- You can also tell your friends and family how important bees are and write to people who make rules about pesticides to let them know we need to protect the bees!

Let's Save the Bees!

Bees do so much for us—they help grow the food we eat and make the world beautiful. Now it's our turn to help them. By working together, we can give bees a chance to keep buzzing around for many years to come!

The Amazing Polar Bear: King of the Arctic

Have you ever seen a polar bear? These big, fluffy white bears live far, far away in a super cold place called the Arctic, near the North Pole. Our penguin friends live way down at the bottom of the Earth, so they never get to meet the polar bears!

A Very Special Bear

The polar bear is the biggest land predator, but guess what? It's actually a marine mammal! This means it spends most of its time swimming in the icy Arctic Ocean. Polar bears are great swimmers and can swim really fast! They don't have any natural enemies, so no one hunts them.

Polar Bears and Brown Bears: Cousins?

Polar bears are related to brown bears! A long time ago, about 150,000 years ago, some brown bears got stuck in giant sheets of ice called glaciers. They had to get used to the freezing Arctic, and over time, they turned into the polar bears we know today!

Did you know that polar bears and brown bears can have babies together? Their babies are called "pizzlies" or "grolar bears!"

What Do Polar Bears Eat?

Polar bears love to eat seals! Seals munch on fish that are full of yummy oils and vitamins. When a polar bear catches a seal, it saves all that good nutrition, especially in its liver. But guess what? A polar bear's liver has so much vitamin A that it would be dangerous for people to eat!

Polar Bears: Arctic Survivors

Living in the super cold Arctic, polar bears have special features to help them survive. Their thick, colorless fur keeps them warm, and their skin underneath is black, which helps soak up the sun's heat. They also have a thick layer of fat to keep them warm and store energy.

Polar bears even have furry pads on their feet to help them walk on ice without slipping. They are always looking for food, and unlike some bears, polar bears don't hibernate—they stay active all year!

The Arctic Hunter

Polar bears are great hunters! They wait on the ice for seals to come up for air, and when the time is right, they strike! They can run fast on land and swim quickly in the icy water, making them awesome hunters in the Arctic.

But Are Polar Bears Safe?

With all their amazing abilities, you might think polar bears are safe, but things aren't always what they seem. The world is getting warmer, and the ice where polar bears live is melting. Without ice, it's harder for them to find seals, and that makes life very tough for them.

We can help polar bears by learning about them and doing our part to protect their icy homes. These incredible creatures remind us how beautiful and delicate our planet is. Let's do what we can to keep the Arctic wild and free for polar bears!

That's the story of the polar bear—an amazing animal that rules the frozen north. Wouldn't it be cool to see one up close (from a safe distance, of course)? Remember, every little thing we do to help the environment helps the animals that live in it too!

The Amazing Bears: From Polar to Pizzly!

Did you know that bears have been around for a super long time—like 40 to 50 million years? That's a lot! Long ago, during the ice age, some bears lived in the cold, icy North, while others moved south to cozy, green forests. Let's go on an adventure into the awesome world of bears!

Polar Bears: Kings of the Ice

The bears that stayed in the Arctic became known as polar bears. These cool animals have thick, white fur to keep them warm and help them hide in the snow. Can you imagine chasing a slippery seal on the ice? Polar bears can do that! Their paws have little bumps that help them grip the snow, so they don't slip.

Polar bears have super sharp teeth to catch their food—mostly seals! But here's a funny fact: the polar bear's liver has so much vitamin A that it would make people sick if we tried to eat it! So while polar bears enjoy their meals, we need to be careful with our vitamins!

Grizzly Bears: Masters of the Forest

Meanwhile, some bears traveled south to live in forests. These bears are called grizzly bears or brown bears. Their dark brown fur helps them hide among the trees. Grizzlies have strong claws for climbing and digging, and they are great hunters, too!

A Surprising Journey

As the ice in the Arctic started to melt, polar bears found it harder to catch seals. They began wandering south to find food. Can you believe that some polar bears ended up in a little village in Northern Russia? The villagers saw as many as 50 polar bears! To keep the kids safe, they had to put guards around their school!

At the same time, grizzly bears were moving north, following the paths of caribou.

A Wild Encounter

What happens when polar bears and grizzly bears meet? In 2006, a hunter thought he saw a white polar bear, but surprise! It had long claws and some brown fur. Scientists found out it was the first pizzly bear ever! A pizzly bear is a special mix of a polar bear and a grizzly bear.

In 2010, another pizzly was discovered. Guess what? Its dad was a grizzly, and its mom was a pizzly! This was super exciting because it meant pizzly bears could have their own babies!

New Bears for a New World

As our planet changes, new bear types like the pizzly bear are popping up. Who knows what other surprises are waiting for us in the wild? The story of bears teaches us about how animals change to survive.

So next time you think of bears, remember the journeys of polar bears, grizzly bears, and the amazing pizzly bear! What a fantastic world we live in!

The Very Important Vultures

Have you ever seen a vulture flying high in the sky? These big birds are super important! Vultures come in different types—there are 23 kinds! Some live in places like Europe and Africa, and some live in America.

What Do Vultures Do?

Vultures love to eat something called carrion, which is a fancy word for the remains of dead animals. It might sound yucky, but vultures help keep our world clean! By eating carrion, they stop bad germs from spreading. Vultures are like nature's cleanup crew!

Sometimes, people mix up vultures with buzzards. But buzzards are hunting birds that catch live animals. One of the birds you might hear about is the turkey buzzard, which is actually a type of vulture!

A Trip to India

A long time ago, I went to a place called India and saw lots of vultures flying around. India had about 80 million vultures—wow, that's a lot! But then something sad happened. Farmers gave their cows a medicine that made vultures sick when they ate the dead cows. This made a lot of vultures die.

Before the medicine was banned, the vulture population dropped from 80 million to just a few thousand. Can you imagine losing that many vultures?

Why Are Vultures So Important?

Without vultures, other animals like rats and wild dogs started eating the dead animals. This caused more rats and wild dogs, which can spread sickness to people.

Vultures in Danger

Now, many vultures are in danger. In Africa, vultures are getting hurt by poisons meant for other animals. In some places, bad people hurt vultures because they could tell the police where they are.

Sadly, 9 kinds of vultures are now endangered, which means they could disappear forever if we don't protect them.

What Can We Do to Help?

The good news is that people are trying to save vultures. Some scientists are catching vultures to help them have more babies. But we all need to help!

Did you know that in some countries, they still use that bad medicine? If we don't stop it, vultures might disappear just like they did in India.

If you want to help, you can learn more about vultures and how to protect them!

Why Should We Care?

Vultures may not be the prettiest birds, but they are very important for keeping our planet healthy. If we don't take care of them, we could have even bigger problems with sickness.

Let's remember to care for vultures and all the amazing animals on our planet!

Giraffes: The Gentle Giants

Giraffes are really cool animals, and people have loved them for a long time! Even way back when a man named Julius Caesar was in charge of Rome, he showed giraffes to people because they were so special. Today, we still think giraffes are amazing. You might have even seen a giraffe at the zoo or as a toy mascot!

Meet the Tallest Animal

Giraffes are super tall! In fact, they are the tallest animals on land, sometimes growing up to 19 feet tall! That's like having two big cars stacked on top of each other! They have long necks, and inside their necks, there are seven big bones. Just one of these bones is as long as a ruler!

Some scientists think giraffes have long necks so they can eat leaves from tall trees, while others think they use their long necks to fight other giraffes. But the truth is, no one knows for sure why their necks are so long!

Who Are Giraffes' Cousins?

Even though giraffes look so different, they actually have some surprising animal cousins! Giraffes are related to cows and antelopes, which live on farms or in the wild. Isn't that surprising?

Giraffes Need Our Help

Sadly, giraffes are in trouble. There aren't as many giraffes in the world as there used to be, and some people hurt them by hunting. But guess what? You can help giraffes! Even though you're small, you can do big things to protect animals.

Protecting Animals

In the United States, there's a special law called the Endangered Species Act that helps protect animals like giraffes. It's like a shield that keeps animals safe when they're in danger. Some people are working hard to make sure giraffes get added to this list so they can be safe.

What You Can Do

If you love giraffes, you can write a letter to the people who help protect them, telling them how much you care. Your voice is important!

Be a Hero for Animals

All animals, whether they're giraffes in Africa or pets in your neighborhood, need love and protection. You can help by learning about animals, asking questions, and doing what you can to take care of them. Together, we can make sure giraffes and other animals stay safe for a long, long time!

The Great Sparrow Story: Why Nature Needs Balance

A long, long time ago, in 1958, the leader of a big country called China, named Mao Zedong, had an idea. He wanted to help farmers grow more food, so he made a plan called the "Four Pests Campaign." In this plan, people were told to get rid of animals that they thought were bad for crops, like rats, flies, mosquitoes, and sparrows. Mao thought sparrows were eating too much of the food people were trying to grow, so he told everyone to chase away and get rid of the sparrows.

People all over China scared the sparrows, destroyed their nests, and soon there were hardly any sparrows left. They thought with the sparrows gone, they would have more food. But guess what? Sparrows weren't just eating the food—they were also eating bugs called locusts, which can be very bad for plants.

Without the sparrows, the locusts started to take over! Huge groups of locusts ate all the crops, and at the same time, China had droughts and floods, which made it even harder for food to grow. Because there wasn't enough food, many people didn't have anything to eat, and lots of people got very hungry. It was a very sad time, and many people died because they didn't have enough food.

This story teaches us how important it is to keep nature in balance. Every animal, even little ones like sparrows, has a special job to do. If we try to get rid of too many animals, it can make big problems for everyone. Now we know that we need to protect all animals and take care of nature.

Today, there are lots of animals, like sharks and rays, that need our help. If we don't protect them, it could cause even bigger problems in the future. Every animal, no matter how small, helps keep the world working the way it should!

The Fun World of Pigeons

Once upon a time, there was a bird you've probably seen before—the pigeon! Pigeons live in cities, sit on rooftops, and love looking for crumbs to eat. But did you know pigeons are super cool and have an amazing story? Let's go on a fun adventure to learn all about pigeons!

A Long, Long Time Ago…

About 5,000 years ago, people started keeping pigeons to carry messages. There were no phones or emails back then, so pigeons helped by flying notes from one place to another. Over time, people noticed that pigeons looked different. Some were dark, some had spots, and some had cool patterns on their wings. People thought it was fun to see what new colors and patterns they could make!

Pigeon Wing Patterns

Did you know pigeons have different wing patterns? Some have spots or stripes on their wings that help them blend into the city. The most common pattern is called "checkered." But there's something even cooler! Some pigeons have no bars or patterns at all, and that's super rare. Scientists discovered that these special pigeons might have the same gene that causes some people to have trouble seeing. Studying pigeons could help us learn more about humans, too!

The Colors of Pigeons

Pigeons come in three main colors: ash red, blue/black, and brown. Most pigeons are blue/black, and you can see them almost anywhere! Brown pigeons are special because they are very rare. Even though ash red is the strongest color, you don't see too many red pigeons flying around. Scientists think darker pigeons may be better at hiding from animals that want to eat them. Isn't that interesting?

Pigeons and a Scientist Named Charles Darwin

Now, let's talk about a famous man named Charles Darwin. He was born the same day as Abraham Lincoln! Darwin studied animals, and pigeons were one of his favorites. He noticed how pigeons could change over time, with different colors and patterns. This helped him come up with a big idea: animals change over time to survive better in their homes.

Pigeons and Nature

Today, scientists still believe Darwin's ideas about how animals change to fit their world. So the next time you see a pigeon, remember how special they are. Pigeons have been helping people for thousands of years and might even help us learn more about nature in the future!

The End.

The Fun World of Pigeons

Once upon a time, there was a bird you've probably seen before—the pigeon! Pigeons live in cities, sit on rooftops, and love looking for crumbs to eat. But did you know pigeons are super cool and have an amazing story? Let's go on a fun adventure to learn all about pigeons!

A Long, Long Time Ago...

About 5,000 years ago, people started keeping pigeons to carry messages. There were no phones or emails back then, so pigeons helped by flying notes from one place to another. Over time, people noticed that pigeons looked different. Some were dark, some had spots, and some had cool patterns on their wings. People thought it was fun to see what new colors and patterns they could make!

Pigeon Wing Patterns

Did you know pigeons have different wing patterns? Some have spots or stripes on their wings that help them blend into the city. The most common pattern is called "checkered." But there's something even cooler! Some pigeons have no bars or patterns at all, and that's super rare. Scientists discovered that these special pigeons might have the same gene that causes some people to have trouble seeing. Studying pigeons could help us learn more about humans, too!

The Colors of Pigeons

Pigeons come in three main colors: ash red, blue/black, and brown. Most pigeons are blue/black, and you can see them almost anywhere! Brown pigeons are special because they are very rare. Even though ash red is the strongest color, you don't see too many red pigeons flying around. Scientists think darker pigeons may be better at hiding from animals that want to eat them. Isn't that interesting?

Pigeons and a Scientist Named Charles Darwin

Now, let's talk about a famous man named Charles Darwin. He was born the same day as Abraham Lincoln! Darwin studied animals, and pigeons were one of his favorites. He noticed how pigeons could change over time, with different colors and patterns. This helped him come up with a big idea: animals change over time to survive better in their homes.

Pigeons and Nature

Today, scientists still believe Darwin's ideas about how animals change to fit their world. So the next time you see a pigeon, remember how special they are. Pigeons have been helping people for thousands of years and might even help us learn more about nature in the future!

The End.

Why Big Animals Are Important: Keeping Nature Happy

Have you ever seen a puzzle? Each piece fits together just right, and when one piece is missing, the whole picture changes. Nature is like a big puzzle too! All the animals, plants, and even tiny things we can't see work together. When we take away one animal, it can make a big difference for everyone else.

The Story of Wolves and Coyotes

A long time ago, in a place with lots of grass and trees, there were many animals. Rabbits ate the grass, coyotes hunted the rabbits, and wolves hunted big animals like deer. Everything was in balance, like a puzzle that fits perfectly.

But then, people started thinking wolves were scary because they might hurt farm animals. So, they got rid of most of the wolves. But without the wolves, there were too many coyotes. The coyotes couldn't find enough wild animals to eat, so they started eating pets and farm animals instead!

Now, people are thinking, "Should we bring wolves back to help fix the balance?"

The Ocean's Big Fish and Sharks

Let's visit the ocean! In the ocean, sharks are the big bosses. Sharks eat big fish, big fish eat medium fish, and medium fish eat little fish. The little fish eat something super tiny called plankton. Plankton are like the trees of the ocean because they help make the air we breathe!

But what if all the sharks went away? Then the big fish would eat too many medium fish, and the medium fish would eat too many little fish. Without enough little fish, the plankton would disappear. And without plankton, we'd have less clean air to breathe. That's why sharks are so important!

The Story of Cats and Rats

Here's a story about cats and rats! A long time ago in Europe, people thought black cats were bad luck, so they got rid of lots of cats. But without cats to catch the rats, there were suddenly too many rats!

Rats carried tiny bugs called fleas, and these fleas made people very sick. Many, many people got sick because there were too many rats. If they had kept the cats around, the rats wouldn't have spread the sickness so fast.

Why Big Animals Matter

Big animals like wolves, sharks, and even tigers are very important. They help keep everything in balance. If we take them away, it messes up the whole puzzle. When nature is balanced, plants and animals stay happy—and so do we!

That's why it's important to protect all the animals, especially the big ones. They help keep the world working just right!

The End.

The Wolf: A Special Animal

A long time ago, people didn't like wolves very much. In lots of stories, wolves were called mean names and thought to be scary. In one story from a place called Norway, a wolf named Fenrir was called a monster! In other places, people thought wolves were sneaky or even bad guys in disguise.

Have you heard the story of the "Big Bad Wolf"? It's just a story, but it made many people think wolves were scary. Even today, some people still think wolves are bad animals. But guess what? Wolves are not as scary as the stories make them seem!

Wolves Are Not So Bad

Wolves hunt to find food, just like bears and foxes do. Sometimes, wolves might eat farm animals, but they don't want to hurt people. It's very rare for wolves to hurt humans. So, why do people think wolves are bad? Maybe it's because of all those stories, but in real life, wolves are very special animals.

Some people even use the word "wolf" in funny ways that don't make sense. Have you ever heard someone whistle when they see something they like? That's called a "wolf whistle," but wolves don't act like that at all! Wolves are actually very loyal. They stay with the same partner for life, which is better than some people!

Wolves Love Their Families

Wolves live in groups called packs. Only the mom and dad wolf in the pack have babies, called pups. The mother wolf hunts with the pack and brings food back for her pups. Wolves take care of each other and will even protect their family from danger. Sometimes, a wolf will be so brave that it risks its life to keep its family safe.

There's a famous story from a long time ago about two brothers named Romulus and Remus. They were raised by wolves and later became the founders of the city of Rome! Because of this story, the wolf is still the national animal of Italy today.

Wolves Are Super Smart

Wolves are very smart and work as a team. When they hunt together, they can catch animals that are bigger than them, like elk! That's why the University of Nevada's sports team is called the "Wolf Pack"—because wolves are loyal, smart, and brave.

Wolves and Dogs Are Family

Did you know that wolves are closely related to dogs? Even tiny dogs, like Chihuahuas, are related to wolves! Long ago, wolves from a place called Israel passed on their special tiny size to little dogs. It's a mystery how these tiny dogs made their way to places like Guatemala, but it might have been sailors bringing them across the ocean on their ships.

Wolves Are Important

Wolves are caring, strong, and loyal. They are the wild cousins of the dogs we love today. Sadly, there are not as many wolves as there used to be. Once, there were over 2 million wolves, but now, there are only about 200,000 left in the wild.

Wolves are not the "big, bad" creatures from fairy tales. They are important animals, and we need to help protect them!

The End.

The Amazing Duck-Billed Platypus

The duck-billed platypus is a super cool animal from Australia! It's really special because it's a mammal, but it lays eggs like a bird. Let's find out more about this amazing creature!

What Does It Look Like?

The platypus looks like it's made from parts of different animals! It has thick fur to keep warm in the water, and the top of its fur is brown while its belly is lighter. It has a flat tail like a beaver's, which helps it swim and store food. A grown-up platypus is about as long as a cat!

But the funniest thing about the platypus is its big, soft bill, which looks like a duck's! It uses the bill to find food underwater by feeling tiny movements. The platypus can even use its bill to dig a burrow to live in!

A Great Swimmer

The platypus loves to swim! It has webbed feet that help it move easily in rivers. It's so good at swimming that it can close its eyes, ears, and nose to keep the water out. The platypus is mostly active at night, but sometimes it swims during the day, too. It likes to be alone and keeps other animals away from its space.

What Does It Eat?

Even though the platypus looks cute, it eats meat! But don't worry—it only eats tiny creatures like bugs, worms, and crabs. The platypus dives underwater to find food with its bill. It picks up mud and spits out the dirt, keeping the food in its mouth. Sometimes it even saves food in its cheeks!

Saving the Platypus

Sadly, there aren't as many platypuses as there used to be because their homes are being destroyed, and the water is getting dirty. But people are trying to help by protecting their homes and keeping the water clean.

The duck-billed platypus is an amazing animal with traits from different kinds of creatures, making it one of the coolest animals in nature! We can help protect the platypus so it can live for a long, long time!

The Marvelous Monarch Butterfly

The monarch butterfly is a beautiful insect with bright orange and black wings. You can find them in places like North America, Mexico, and even parts of South America! Monarchs are super special and remind us how amazing nature is.

Life of a Monarch

A monarch butterfly's life begins as a tiny egg on a milkweed leaf. When the egg hatches, a baby caterpillar, called a larva, comes out. These caterpillars love to eat only one thing—milkweed!

After eating and growing bigger, the caterpillar makes a special shell called a chrysalis. Inside the chrysalis, something magical happens! The caterpillar changes into a butterfly in a process called metamorphosis. Once the butterfly is ready, it comes out of the chrysalis and flies away!

A Journey Like No Other

Monarch butterflies are famous for their long trips, called migration. When the weather gets colder, they fly to warmer places in the south, like Mexico, traveling thousands of miles! When spring comes, they fly back to where they started. This long journey is one of the coolest things in nature!

Saving the Monarchs

Monarch butterflies are in danger because their homes are being destroyed, and milkweed plants are disappearing. But people are helping! Groups are working hard to protect monarch butterflies and their homes so they can stay with us.

The monarch butterfly shows us how wonderful nature is and why it's important to take care of our planet. Let's help protect these amazing butterflies!

Save the White Rhino!

The rhinoceros, or rhino for short, is one of the biggest animals on Earth—only elephants are bigger! There are two types of rhinos: the black rhino and the white rhino. The white rhino has two kinds, called the northern white rhino and the southern white rhino.

Why Are Rhinos Disappearing?

Rhinos are in trouble because of people. Some people hunt them for their horns, which can be sold for a lot of money—up to $400,000! That's even more than gold! Because so many rhinos are being hunted, it's hard for them to stay alive. Right now, there are only two northern white rhinos left in the whole world, and they are both girls!

Can We Save the Rhinos?

But don't worry, there is still hope! Before the last boy northern white rhino passed away, scientists saved his special cells and froze them. This means they might be able to help make baby rhinos one day!

There's another problem, though. There might not be any healthy eggs left from the girl rhinos to make new baby rhinos. Scientists are trying to fix this by using something called stem cells, which are special cells that can turn into different types of cells, like the kind that makes eggs.

Stem cells can also help scientists find cures for illnesses and might even help people walk again!

The Big Question

While scientists are doing wonderful things, some people worry about how stem cells are collected. They come from tiny babies called embryos, and some groups don't agree with that. It's a big discussion about what is right and wrong.

But right now, we can help! We might not be able to bring back animals like woolly mammoths, but we can stop people from hunting rhinos and protect the ones we have!

Let's all work together to save the rhinos before it's too late!

The Turtle Mystery!

Once upon a time, people thought all scientists agreed on everything. But guess what? That's not true at all! Scientists often have different ideas, especially about animals. And one big mystery today is about turtles!

How Did Scientists Think?

For a long time, scientists called biologists (that's what we call scientists who study living things) grouped animals by how they looked. So, animals that looked similar, like turtles and lizards, were put in the same group. Most scientists thought turtles were close relatives of snakes and lizards.

A New Idea!

Then something amazing happened! New scientists called molecular biologists started looking at animals in a different way. Instead of just looking at how animals looked, they studied tiny building blocks inside living things called proteins. They thought animals with similar proteins were more closely related, even if they didn't look alike!

The Turtle Surprise

In 2012, a scientist named Ylenia Chiari had a surprising idea. She wondered if turtles might be more like birds than snakes or lizards. Can you believe it? Turtles and birds, best buddies!

To find out, a group of scientists studied a special protein in the blood of a Galapagos tortoise, which is one of the biggest turtles in the world. They compared the turtle's protein to those in other animals using a super-smart computer. It was like a matching game for animals!

Here's what they found:

- The Galapagos tortoise's protein matched closely with other turtles, of course.

- But next in line? Birds like ducks, penguins, and chickens! That's right, chickens!

- They even found that turtles share some proteins with elephants and... people like you and me!

What Does This Mean?

The results were pretty clear: turtles are more closely related to birds than to lizards when we look at their proteins. It's almost like the turtle's secret family tree goes back to birds, not reptiles!

And here's something else to think about: If humans, turtles, birds, and even elephants share some of the same proteins, doesn't that mean all living creatures are connected? Maybe that's a great reason for us to treat all animals with kindness and respect.

The world of science is full of mysteries, and sometimes the answers are even more surprising than we think!

Save the Manatee!

Meet the manatee, a gentle giant of the sea! These amazing creatures are big and slow, and they love to swim in warm, coastal waters. Just like us, manatees are mammals, which means they breathe air and take care of their babies.

What Do Manatees Eat?

Adult manatees can weigh between 1,200 and 1,500 pounds—wow! That's like having a small car swimming in the ocean! Every day, they munch on up to 150 pounds of plants, mainly seagrass that grows on the ocean floor. They love eating these tasty greens so much that sailors long ago might have mistaken them for mermaids!

Protecting Our Gentle Giants

Even though manatees don't have any natural predators, they still need our help. There's a special law called the Marine Mammals

Protection Act that makes it illegal to hurt them. You'd think that with no predators and lots of food, there would be plenty of manatees, but sadly, that's not true. In 2021, more than 1,100 manatees died, mostly from starvation caused by pollution.

Manatees in Florida

Most manatees can be found in the warm lagoons of Florida. A lagoon is a special kind of water separated from the ocean by sand or coral. These calm waters are great for swimming, but they also attract lots of boats and fishermen, which can be dangerous for our slow-moving friends.

Manatees aren't very fast, and they have only six neck bones instead of the seven that most mammals have. This makes it hard for them to turn their heads and look around! They come up for air every five minutes, but sometimes they accidentally pop up right in front of speedy boats and jet skis. Many manatees get hurt in accidents or get stuck in fishing nets.

The Real Danger: Starvation

The biggest problem for manatees is actually starvation. Florida is a beautiful place where many plants grow well because of fertilizers that people use in their gardens. But when it rains, these chemicals wash into the lagoons and cause harmful algae to grow too much. This is called an algae bloom.

Normally, manatees would eat seagrass, but these algae blooms block sunlight from reaching the plants below, causing the seagrass to die. Without their favorite food, manatees become hungry and weak.

How You Can Help!

If we want to save the manatees, we need to take action! The United States Fish and Wildlife Department and the State of Florida are working together to fix the pollution problems. Three environmental groups are even taking steps to protect manatee homes!

If you want to help, you can support these organizations:

- **Center for Biological Diversity**
378 Main Street
Tucson, AZ 85701
- **Defenders of Wildlife**
1130 17th Street NW
Washington, DC 20036
- **Save the Manatee Club**
533 Versailles Dr., Ste 100
Maitland, FL 32751

Let's team up to save the manatees and keep our oceans clean! Remember, it's important to care for our planet and all its creatures, big and small!

The Legend of Bigfoot: A Fun Mystery

Have you ever heard of Bigfoot? Bigfoot is a big, hairy creature that people have been telling stories about for a very long time! Some people think Bigfoot is real, and some people don't. But why do so many people keep talking about this giant creature?

A Really Old Story

The story of Bigfoot is super old! Over 1,000 years ago, a man named Leif Erikson came to America and said he saw a giant, hairy man in the woods. And guess what? Native Americans in California also told stories about a big, hairy man, and they even drew pictures of him on rocks. Isn't that cool?

People Still See Bigfoot

Even today, people say they see Bigfoot! In 2022, someone in South Carolina said they saw a big, hairy creature in a park. A man named Dennis found giant footprints that looked like other footprints found in faraway mountains! People have been seeing Bigfoot for a long time, all over the country.

A Big Book About Bigfoot

Did you know that the government even wrote about Bigfoot? In 1975, a book about nature in Washington State talked about Bigfoot, or Sasquatch. They said Bigfoot could be 8 to 12 feet tall and as heavy as a small car! People say Bigfoot has long hair and big feet, and it might eat plants and some meat.

The Bigfoot Mystery

Bigfoot is very shy and doesn't leave many clues behind. Sometimes, people find giant footprints, and there's even a short movie of a creature that might be Bigfoot! Some people think the movie is fake, but others believe it's real.

So, what do you think? Is Bigfoot real, or is it just a fun story? We don't know for sure, and that's what makes it such a great mystery! Keep your mind open and have fun exploring the unknown!

The Mystery of the Chihuahua and the Sailors

Have you ever seen a tiny Chihuahua and thought it looked like a wolf? It's true! Chihuahuas, like all dogs, are related to wolves. Scientists study dog genes to learn more about where different dogs come from. But how did the little Chihuahua get so small?

The Secret in Their Genes

Did you know all dogs, even big ones like Great Danes, share almost the same DNA? There's a special gene in small dogs that keeps them tiny, and it's called IGF-1! This gene tells their bodies to stay small, so Chihuahuas don't grow as big as other dogs.

But why did Chihuahuas get so tiny? Long ago, people like the Mayans may have bred wolves to make smaller dogs. Another idea is that when Spanish people came to America, their dogs mixed with the local dogs. And then there's the Ancient Sailor idea—let's talk about that!

The Ancient Sailor Idea

Some people think that sailors from far away, maybe near Israel, came to Mexico a long, long time ago—around 600 BC! These sailors might have brought their small dogs with them. Those dogs could have mixed with the dogs in Mexico, and over time, they became the Chihuahuas we know today.

Other Small Dogs With Secrets

Chihuahuas aren't the only small dogs with special genes. There are other dogs, like the Mexican Hairless and Chinese Crested, that don't have much hair. They all share a special gene that makes them hairless. How did these hairless dogs end up in different countries? Maybe ancient sailors took them on their long trips!

A Long Journey Over the Sea

If those ancient sailors really did visit, it could help explain how tiny dogs like Chihuahuas came to be. People have even found old artwork showing small dogs from long ago! Maybe sailors shared their dogs when they visited new places, bringing these little friends across the sea.

What's the Best Explanation?

There are many ideas about where Chihuahuas came from, but sometimes the simplest answer is the best. Could it be that ancient sailors brought their little dogs across the ocean, helping make the Chihuahua we see today? Science hasn't solved the mystery yet, but one thing is for sure—every Chihuahua has a big story!

Introducción: ¡Una aventura divertida para ayudar a nuestros amigos animales!

¡Bienvenido a un mundo mágico lleno de animales increíbles! En este libro conoceremos a algunos amigos muy especiales: ¡animales en peligro de extinción! Estos animales, como el manatí manatí y el tigre fuerte, son muy importantes para nuestro planeta. ¡Pero ahora mismo necesitan nuestra ayuda para mantenerse seguros y felices!

Emprenderás un divertido viaje alrededor del mundo para aprender todo sobre estos increíbles animales. Descubriremos dónde viven, qué les gusta hacer y por qué necesitan nuestra ayuda. ¡Prepárate para conocer datos interesantes, historias dulces y muchas formas en las que puedes ser un héroe para ellos!

¡Cada capítulo te hablará de un animal diferente en peligro de extinción, como el gran y amigable manatí que nada en el mar! Descubrirás cómo estos nadadores lentos comen deliciosas hierbas marinas y qué sucede cuando sus casas se ensucian. También aprenderemos sobre cosas como la contaminación y cómo podemos ayudar a mantener a nuestros amigos animales seguros y saludables.

Mientras lees, recuerda que incluso las pequeñas cosas que hagas pueden ayudar. ¡Contarles a tus amigos sobre estos animales, ayudar a grupos que los protegen o cuidar nuestra Tierra son excelentes maneras de marcar la diferencia!

¡Entonces, saltemos a las emocionantes historias de estos animales especiales y seamos sus héroes! Juntos podemos asegurarnos de que permanezcan seguros y felices en nuestro planeta durante mucho, mucho tiempo. ¿Estás listo para la aventura? ¡Vamos!

El rumor sobre las abejas: por qué necesitamos salvar a nuestros amigos peludos

¡Hola! ¿Alguna vez has visto una abeja? ¿Esos pequeños insectos zumbadores que vuelan alrededor de las flores? Bueno, ¿adivinen qué? Las abejas son muy importantes para nuestro mundo y hacen mucho más que solo producir miel. Ayudan a que las plantas crezcan y, sin ellos, ¡podríamos tener grandes problemas!

Por qué las abejas son especiales

¿Sabías que las abejas ayudan a que crezcan alrededor del 85% de todas las flores? ¡Esos son casi todos! Van a las flores para recolectar un delicioso néctar y, mientras están allí, ayudan a las flores a producir frutas y verduras. ¡Imagínese ir a la tienda y no encontrar nada de comida! ¡Eso podría pasar si no hubiera abejas!

Un hombre muy inteligente llamado Albert Einstein dijo una vez: "Si la abeja desapareciera de la tierra, a la gente no le quedarían más de cuatro años de vida". ¡Ay! ¡Eso da miedo! Es porque, sin las abejas, no tendríamos suficiente comida para comer.

La danza de la miel

¡Las abejas son pequeñas trabajadoras ocupadas! Hacen miel y la guardan para el invierno. ¿Pero adivina cómo encuentran comida? ¡Hacen un pequeño baile! ¡Es cierto! Cuando una abeja encuentra las mejores flores, baila para decirles a sus amigas adónde ir. Para producir sólo medio kilo de miel, las abejas tienen que visitar entre 2 y 4 millones de flores. ¡Eso es mucho volar y bailar!

Mientras hacen todo eso, también ayudan a que nuestras frutas y verduras crezcan al llevar el polen de flor en flor. Sin las abejas, sería mucho más difícil encontrar cosas deliciosas como manzanas, fresas e incluso zanahorias.

¿Están las abejas en problemas?

¡Ahora mismo, las abejas están en un gran problema! Su número está disminuyendo debido a algo llamado pesticidas. Estos son productos químicos que la gente rocía sobre las plantas para mantener alejados a los insectos dañinos, pero a veces también dañan a las abejas. Un tipo de pesticida, llamado pesticida neonicotínico, es especialmente dañino. ¡Desde 2004, la población de abejas se ha reducido a la mitad!

Si las abejas siguen desapareciendo, podríamos quedarnos sin comida. ¡Necesitamos abejas y ellas necesitan nuestra ayuda!

¿Cómo podemos ayudar a las abejas?

La buena noticia es que hay muchas maneras en que podemos ayudar a salvar a las abejas:

- Si vives en un patio trasero, puedes colocar una colmena de abejas en él para brindarles un hogar seguro.

- Si tienes un jardín pequeño, puedes plantar flores que les gusten a las abejas, ¡como la lavanda!

- Antes de usar cualquier repelente de insectos, verifique si es seguro para las abejas. ¡Puedes buscarlo en línea!

- ¡También puedes contarles a tus amigos y familiares lo importantes que son las abejas y escribirles a las personas que establecen reglas sobre pesticidas para informarles que debemos proteger a las abejas!

¡Salvemos a las abejas!

Las abejas hacen mucho por nosotros: ayudan a cultivar los alimentos que comemos y a embellecer el mundo. Ahora es nuestro turno de ayudarlos. ¡Trabajando juntos, podemos darles a las abejas la oportunidad de seguir zumbando durante muchos años más!

El asombroso oso polar: rey del Ártico

¿Alguna vez has visto un oso polar? Estos osos blancos grandes y peludos viven muy, muy lejos, en un lugar súper frío llamado Ártico, cerca del Polo Norte. Nuestros amigos pingüinos viven en el fondo de la Tierra, por lo que nunca llegan a conocer a los osos polares.

Un oso muy especial

El oso polar es el mayor depredador terrestre, pero ¿adivinen qué? ¡En realidad es un mamífero marino! Esto significa que pasa la mayor parte de su tiempo nadando en el helado Océano Ártico. ¡Los osos polares son grandes nadadores y pueden nadar muy rápido! No tienen enemigos naturales, por lo que nadie los caza.

Osos polares y osos pardos: ¿primos?

¡Los osos polares están relacionados con los osos pardos! Hace mucho tiempo, hace unos 150.000 años, algunos osos pardos quedaron atrapados en gigantescas capas de hielo llamadas glaciares. Tuvieron que acostumbrarse al gélido Ártico y, con el tiempo, ¡se convirtieron en los osos polares que conocemos hoy!

¿Sabías que los osos polares y los osos pardos pueden tener crías juntos? ¡A sus bebés se les llama "pizzlies" u "osos grolar!"

¿Qué comen los osos polares?

¡A los osos polares les encanta comer focas! Las focas comen pescado lleno de deliciosos aceites y vitaminas. Cuando un oso polar atrapa una foca, guarda toda esa buena nutrición, especialmente en su hígado. ¿Pero adivina qué? ¡El hígado de un oso polar tiene tanta vitamina A que sería peligroso para la gente comerlo!

Osos polares: supervivientes del Ártico

Al vivir en el Ártico súper frío, los osos polares tienen características especiales que les ayudan a sobrevivir. Su pelaje espeso e incoloro los mantiene calientes y su piel debajo es negra, lo que les ayuda a absorber el calor del sol. También tienen una gruesa capa de grasa para mantenerlos calientes y almacenar energía.

Los osos polares incluso tienen almohadillas peludas en las patas que les ayudan a caminar sobre el hielo sin resbalar. Siempre están buscando comida y, a diferencia de algunos osos, los osos polares no hibernan: ¡permanecen activos todo el año!

El cazador ártico

¡Los osos polares son grandes cazadores! Esperan en el hielo a que las focas salgan a tomar aire y, cuando llega el momento, ¡atacan! Pueden correr rápido en tierra y nadar rápidamente en agua helada, lo que los convierte en increíbles cazadores en el Ártico.

Pero, ¿están seguros los osos polares?

Con todas sus asombrosas habilidades, uno podría pensar que los osos polares están a salvo, pero las cosas no siempre son lo que parecen. El mundo se está calentando y el hielo donde viven los osos polares se está derritiendo. Sin hielo, les resulta más difícil encontrar focas, y eso les dificulta la vida.

Podemos ayudar a los osos polares aprendiendo sobre ellos y haciendo nuestra parte para proteger sus hogares helados. Estas increíbles criaturas nos recuerdan lo hermoso y delicado que es nuestro planeta.

¡Hagamos lo que podamos para mantener el Ártico salvaje y libre para los osos polares!

Esa es la historia del oso polar, un animal asombroso que gobierna el norte helado. ¿No sería genial ver uno de cerca (desde una distancia segura, por supuesto)? Recuerda, ¡cada pequeña cosa que hacemos para ayudar al medio ambiente también ayuda a los animales que viven en él!

Los Ositos Asombrosos: ¡De Polar a Pizzly!

¿Sabías que los osos existen desde hace mucho tiempo, entre 40 y 50 millones de años? ¡Eso es mucho! Hace mucho tiempo, durante la edad de hielo, algunos osos vivían en el frío y helado norte, mientras que otros se trasladaban al sur, a bosques verdes y acogedores. ¡Embárcate en una aventura en el asombroso mundo de los osos!

Osos polares: reyes del hielo

Los osos que permanecieron en el Ártico pasaron a ser conocidos como osos polares. Estos animales geniales tienen un pelaje blanco y espeso para mantenerlos abrigados y ayudarlos a esconderse en la nieve. ¿Te imaginas perseguir una foca resbaladiza sobre el hielo? ¡Los osos polares pueden hacer eso! Sus patas tienen pequeñas protuberancias que les ayudan a agarrarse a la nieve y no resbalarse.

Los osos polares tienen dientes súper afilados para atrapar su comida, ¡principalmente focas! Pero he aquí un dato curioso: ¡el hígado del oso polar tiene tanta vitamina A que enfermaría a la gente si intentáramos comérselo! Entonces, mientras los osos polares disfrutan de sus comidas, ¡debemos tener cuidado con nuestras vitaminas!

Osos Grizzly: Maestros del Bosque

Mientras tanto, algunos osos viajaron hacia el sur para vivir en los bosques. Estos osos se llaman osos grizzly u osos pardos. Su pelaje marrón oscuro les ayuda a esconderse entre los árboles. Los osos pardos tienen garras fuertes para trepar y cavar, ¡y también son excelentes cazadores!

Un viaje sorprendente

A medida que el hielo del Ártico comenzó a derretirse, a los osos polares les resultó más difícil cazar focas. Comenzaron a viajar hacia el sur en busca de comida. ¿Puedes creer que unos osos polares terminaron en un pequeño pueblo del norte de Rusia? ¡Los aldeanos vieron hasta 50 osos polares! Para mantener seguros a los niños, ¡tuvieron que poner guardias alrededor de su escuela!

Al mismo tiempo, los osos grizzly se desplazaban hacia el norte, siguiendo los caminos del caribú.

Un encuentro salvaje

¿Qué sucede cuando los osos polares y los osos pardos se encuentran? En 2006, un cazador creyó ver un oso polar blanco, ¡pero sorpresa! Tenía garras largas y algo de pelaje marrón. ¡Los científicos descubrieron que fue el primer oso pizzy de la historia! Un oso pizzly es una mezcla especial de oso polar y oso grizzly.

En 2010, se descubrió otro extraño. ¿Adivina qué? ¡Su papá era un oso pardo y su mamá era una pizzly! ¡Esto fue súper emocionante porque significaba que los osos Pizzly podrían tener sus propios bebés!

Nuevos osos para un nuevo mundo

A medida que nuestro planeta cambia, están apareciendo nuevos tipos de osos como el oso pizzly. ¿Quién sabe qué otras sorpresas nos esperan en la naturaleza? La historia de los osos nos enseña cómo los animales cambian para sobrevivir.

Así que la próxima vez que pienses en osos, recuerda los viajes de los osos polares, los osos grizzly y el increíble oso pizzly. ¡Qué mundo tan fantástico en el que vivimos!

Los buitres muy importantes

¿Alguna vez has visto un buitre volando alto en el cielo? ¡Estos grandes pájaros son súper importantes! Los buitres son de diferentes tipos: ¡hay 23 tipos! Algunos viven en lugares como Europa y África, y otros viven en América.

¿Qué hacen los buitres?

A los buitres les encanta comer algo llamado carroña, que es una palabra elegante para los restos de animales muertos. Puede parecer asqueroso, ¡pero los buitres ayudan a mantener nuestro mundo limpio! Al comer carroña, impiden la propagación de gérmenes nocivos. ¡Los buitres son como el equipo de limpieza de la naturaleza!

A veces, la gente confunde buitres con buitres. Pero los buitres son aves cazadoras que capturan animales vivos. Una de las aves de las que quizás oigas hablar es el ratonero, que en realidad es un tipo de buitre.

Un viaje a la India

Hace mucho tiempo fui a un lugar llamado India y vi muchos buitres volando por ahí. India tenía alrededor de 80 millones de buitres. ¡Vaya, eso es mucho! Pero entonces sucedió algo triste. Los granjeros daban a sus vacas una medicina que enfermaba a los buitres cuando se comían las vacas muertas. Esto hizo que murieran muchos buitres.

Antes de que se prohibiera el medicamento, la población de buitres se redujo de 80 millones a sólo unos pocos miles. ¿Te imaginas perder tantos buitres?

¿Por qué son tan importantes los buitres?

Sin buitres, otros animales como ratas y perros salvajes comenzaron a comerse los animales muertos. Esto provocó más ratas y perros salvajes, que pueden transmitir enfermedades a las personas.

Buitres en peligro

Ahora muchos buitres están en peligro. En África, los buitres están resultando heridos por venenos destinados a otros animales. En algunos lugares, la gente mala lastima a los buitres porque podrían decirle a la policía dónde están.

Lamentablemente, actualmente hay 9 tipos de buitres en peligro de extinción, lo que significa que podrían desaparecer para siempre si no los protegemos.

¿Qué podemos hacer para ayudar?

La buena noticia es que la gente está intentando salvar a los buitres. Algunos científicos están cazando buitres para ayudarles a tener más crías. ¡Pero todos necesitamos ayudar!

¿Sabías que en algunos países todavía se usa esa mala medicina? Si no lo detenemos, los buitres podrían desaparecer tal como ocurrió en la India.

Si quieres ayudar, ¡puedes aprender más sobre los buitres y cómo protegerlos!

¿Por qué debería importarnos?

Puede que los buitres no sean las aves más bonitas, pero son muy importantes para mantener nuestro planeta saludable. Si no los cuidamos, podríamos tener problemas aún mayores de enfermedad.

¡Recordemos cuidar de los buitres y de todos los increíbles animales de nuestro planeta!

Jirafas: los gentiles gigantes

¡Las jirafas son animales realmente geniales y la gente las ama desde hace mucho tiempo! Incluso hace mucho tiempo, cuando un hombre llamado Julio César estaba a cargo de Roma, mostraba jirafas a la gente porque eran muy especiales. Hoy en día, todavía pensamos que las jirafas son asombrosas. ¡Es posible que incluso hayas visto una jirafa en el zoológico o como mascota de juguete!

Conoce al animal más alto

¡Las jirafas son súper altas! De hecho, son los animales más altos en la tierra, ¡a veces crecen hasta 19 pies de altura! ¡Es como tener dos autos grandes apilados uno encima del otro! Tienen cuellos largos y dentro de ellos hay siete huesos grandes. ¡Solo uno de estos huesos es tan largo como una regla!

Algunos científicos creen que las jirafas tienen cuellos largos para poder comer hojas de árboles altos, mientras que otros piensan que usan sus cuellos largos para luchar contra otras jirafas. Pero la verdad es que nadie sabe con certeza por qué sus cuellos son tan largos.

¿Quiénes son los primos de las jirafas?

Aunque las jirafas se ven tan diferentes, ¡en realidad tienen algunos primos animales sorprendentes! Las jirafas están relacionadas con las vacas y los antílopes, que viven en granjas o en la naturaleza. ¿No es sorprendente?

Las jirafas necesitan nuestra ayuda

Lamentablemente, las jirafas están en problemas. Ya no hay tantas jirafas en el mundo como antes y algunas personas las dañan cazando. ¿Pero adivina qué? ¡Tú puedes ayudar a las jirafas! Aunque seas pequeño, puedes hacer grandes cosas para proteger a los animales.

Protegiendo a los animales

En Estados Unidos, existe una ley especial llamada Ley de Especies en Peligro de Extinción que ayuda a proteger a animales como las jirafas. Es como un escudo que mantiene a los animales a salvo cuando están en peligro. Algunas personas están trabajando arduamente para asegurarse de que las jirafas se agreguen a esta lista para que puedan estar a salvo.

Qué puedes hacer

Si amas a las jirafas, puedes escribir una carta a las personas que ayudan a protegerlas, diciéndoles cuánto te importan. ¡Tu voz es importante!

Sea un héroe para los animales

Todos los animales, ya sean jirafas en África o mascotas de tu vecindario, necesitan amor y protección. Puedes ayudar aprendiendo sobre los animales, haciendo preguntas y haciendo lo que puedas para cuidarlos. ¡Juntos podemos asegurarnos de que las jirafas y otros animales permanezcan a salvo durante mucho, mucho tiempo!

La historia del gran gorrión: por qué la naturaleza necesita equilibrio

Hace mucho, mucho tiempo, en 1958, el líder de un gran país llamado China, llamado Mao Zedong, tuvo una idea. Quería ayudar a los agricultores a cultivar más alimentos, por lo que elaboró un plan llamado "Campaña de las cuatro plagas". En este plan, se pidió a las personas que se deshicieran de los animales que pensaban que eran malos para los cultivos, como ratas, moscas, mosquitos y gorriones. Mao pensó que los gorriones estaban comiendo demasiado del alimento que la gente intentaba cultivar, por lo que les dijo a todos que los ahuyentaran y se deshicieran de los gorriones.

La gente de toda China asustó a los gorriones, destruyó sus nidos y pronto ya casi no quedaban gorriones. Pensaron que, sin los gorriones, tendrían más comida. ¿Pero adivina qué? Los gorriones no sólo comían la comida, sino que también comían insectos llamados langostas, que pueden ser muy perjudiciales para las plantas.

¡Sin los gorriones, las langostas comenzaron a apoderarse del país! Enormes grupos de langostas se comieron todos los cultivos y, al mismo tiempo, China sufrió sequías e inundaciones, lo que dificultó aún más el cultivo de alimentos. Debido a que no había suficiente comida, mucha gente no tenía nada que comer y mucha gente tenía mucha hambre. Fue una época muy triste y mucha gente murió por no tener suficiente comida.

Esta historia nos enseña lo importante que es mantener la naturaleza en equilibrio. Cada animal, incluso los más pequeños como los gorriones, tiene un trabajo especial que realizar. Si intentamos deshacernos de demasiados animales, puede generar grandes problemas para todos. Ahora sabemos que debemos proteger a todos los animales y cuidar la naturaleza.

Hoy en día, hay muchos animales, como tiburones y rayas, que necesitan nuestra ayuda. Si no los protegemos, podrían causar problemas aún mayores en el futuro. ¡Cada animal, por pequeño que sea, ayuda a que el mundo funcione como debería!

El divertido mundo de las palomas

Érase una vez un pájaro que probablemente hayas visto antes: ¡la paloma! Las palomas viven en ciudades, se posan en los tejados y les encanta buscar migajas para comer. ¿Pero sabías que las palomas son geniales y tienen una historia asombrosa? ¡Embárcate en una divertida aventura para aprender todo sobre las palomas!

Hace mucho, mucho tiempo...

Hace unos 5.000 años, la gente empezó a criar palomas para llevar mensajes. En aquel entonces no había teléfonos ni correos electrónicos, por lo que las palomas ayudaban volando notas de un lugar a otro. Con el tiempo, la gente notó que las palomas tenían un aspecto diferente. Algunos eran oscuros, otros tenían manchas y algunos tenían patrones fríos en sus alas. ¡La gente pensó que era divertido ver qué nuevos colores y patrones podían hacer!

Patrones de alas de paloma

¿Sabías que las palomas tienen diferentes patrones de alas? Algunos tienen manchas o rayas en las alas que les ayudan a mimetizarse con la ciudad. El patrón más común se llama "a cuadros". ¡Pero hay algo aún más genial! Algunas palomas no tienen barras ni patrones, y eso es muy raro. Los científicos descubrieron que estas palomas especiales podrían tener el mismo gen que hace que algunas personas tengan problemas para ver. ¡Estudiar las palomas también podría ayudarnos a aprender más sobre los humanos!

Los colores de las palomas

Las palomas vienen en tres colores principales: rojo ceniza, azul/negro y marrón. ¡La mayoría de las palomas son azules/negras y puedes verlas en casi cualquier lugar! Las palomas marrones son especiales porque son muy raras. Aunque el rojo ceniza es el color más fuerte, no se ven muchas palomas rojas volando por ahí. Los científicos creen que las palomas más oscuras pueden esconderse mejor de los animales que quieren comérselas. ¿No es interesante?

Palomas y un científico llamado Charles Darwin

Ahora, hablemos de un hombre famoso llamado Charles Darwin. ¡Nació el mismo día que Abraham Lincoln! Darwin estudió animales y las palomas eran una de sus favoritas. Se dio cuenta de cómo las palomas podían cambiar con el tiempo, con diferentes colores y patrones. Esto le ayudó a tener una gran idea: los animales cambian con el tiempo para sobrevivir mejor en sus hogares.

Palomas y naturaleza

Hoy en día, los científicos todavía creen en las ideas de Darwin sobre cómo los animales cambian para adaptarse a su mundo. Así que la próxima vez que veas una paloma, recuerda lo especiales que son. ¡Las palomas han ayudado a las personas durante miles de años e incluso podrían ayudarnos a aprender más sobre la naturaleza en el futuro!

El fin.

El divertido mundo de las palomas

Érase una vez un pájaro que probablemente hayas visto antes: ¡la paloma! Las palomas viven en ciudades, se posan en los tejados y les encanta buscar migajas para comer. ¿Pero sabías que las palomas son geniales y tienen una historia asombrosa? ¡Embárcate en una divertida aventura para aprender todo sobre las palomas!

Hace mucho, mucho tiempo...

Hace unos 5.000 años, la gente empezó a criar palomas para llevar mensajes. En aquel entonces no había teléfonos ni correos electrónicos, por lo que las palomas ayudaban volando notas de un lugar a otro. Con el tiempo, la gente notó que las palomas tenían un aspecto diferente. Algunos eran oscuros, otros tenían manchas y algunos tenían patrones fríos en sus alas. ¡La gente pensó que era divertido ver qué nuevos colores y patrones podían hacer!

Patrones de alas de paloma

¿Sabías que las palomas tienen diferentes patrones de alas? Algunos tienen manchas o rayas en las alas que les ayudan a mimetizarse con la ciudad. El patrón más común se llama "a cuadros". ¡Pero hay algo aún más genial! Algunas palomas no tienen barras ni patrones, y eso es muy raro. Los científicos descubrieron que estas palomas especiales podrían tener el mismo gen que hace que algunas personas tengan problemas para ver. ¡Estudiar las palomas también podría ayudarnos a aprender más sobre los humanos!

Los colores de las palomas

Las palomas vienen en tres colores principales: rojo ceniza, azul/negro y marrón. ¡La mayoría de las palomas son azules/negras y puedes verlas en casi cualquier lugar! Las palomas marrones son especiales porque son muy raras. Aunque el rojo ceniza es el color más fuerte, no se ven muchas palomas rojas volando por ahí. Los científicos creen que las palomas más oscuras pueden esconderse mejor de los animales que quieren comérselas. ¿No es interesante?

Palomas y un científico llamado Charles Darwin

Ahora, hablemos de un hombre famoso llamado Charles Darwin. ¡Nació el mismo día que Abraham Lincoln! Darwin estudió animales y las palomas eran una de sus favoritas. Se dio cuenta de cómo las palomas podían cambiar con el tiempo, con diferentes colores y patrones. Esto le ayudó a tener una gran idea: los animales cambian con el tiempo para sobrevivir mejor en sus hogares.

Palomas y naturaleza

Hoy en día, los científicos todavía creen en las ideas de Darwin sobre cómo los animales cambian para adaptarse a su mundo. Así que la próxima vez que veas una paloma, recuerda lo especiales que son. ¡Las palomas han ayudado a las personas durante miles de años e incluso podrían ayudarnos a aprender más sobre la naturaleza en el futuro!

El fin.

Por qué los animales grandes son importantes: mantener feliz a la naturaleza

¿Alguna vez has visto un rompecabezas? Cada pieza encaja a la perfección, y cuando falta una pieza, la imagen completa cambia. ¡La naturaleza también es como un gran rompecabezas! Todos los animales, plantas e incluso las cosas pequeñas que no podemos ver trabajan juntos. Cuando quitamos un animal, puede marcar una gran diferencia para todos los demás.

La historia de los lobos y los coyotes

Hace mucho tiempo, en un lugar con mucha hierba y árboles, había muchos animales. Los conejos comían la hierba, los coyotes cazaban conejos y los lobos cazaban animales grandes como ciervos. Todo estaba en equilibrio, como un rompecabezas que encaja perfectamente.

Pero entonces, la gente empezó a pensar que los lobos daban miedo porque podían herir a los animales de granja. Entonces se deshicieron de la mayoría de los lobos. Pero sin los lobos, había demasiados coyotes. Los coyotes no pudieron encontrar suficientes animales salvajes para comer, ¡así que comenzaron a comer mascotas y animales de granja!

Ahora la gente piensa: "¿Deberíamos traer lobos de regreso para ayudar a restablecer el equilibrio?"

Los grandes peces y tiburones del océano

¡Visitemos el océano! En el océano, los tiburones son los grandes jefes. Los tiburones comen peces grandes, los peces grandes comen peces medianos y los peces medianos comen peces pequeños. Los peces pequeños comen algo muy pequeño llamado plancton. ¡El plancton es como los árboles del océano porque ayudan a formar el aire que respiramos!

¿Pero qué pasaría si todos los tiburones desaparecieran? Entonces el pez grande se comería demasiados peces medianos y el pez mediano se comería demasiados peces pequeños. Sin suficientes peces, el plancton desaparecería. Y sin plancton, tendríamos menos aire limpio para respirar. ¡Por eso los tiburones son tan importantes!

La historia de los gatos y las ratas

¡Aquí tienes una historia sobre gatos y ratas! Hace mucho tiempo, en Europa, la gente pensaba que los gatos negros traían mala suerte, por lo que se deshicieron de muchos gatos. Pero sin gatos que atraparan a las ratas, ¡de repente había demasiadas ratas!

Las ratas portaban pequeños insectos llamados pulgas, y estas pulgas enfermaban gravemente a la gente. Mucha, mucha gente se enfermó porque había demasiadas ratas. Si hubieran mantenido a los gatos cerca, las ratas no habrían propagado la enfermedad tan rápido.

Por qué son importantes los animales grandes

Los animales grandes como los lobos, los tiburones e incluso los tigres son muy importantes. Ayudan a mantener todo en equilibrio. Si los quitamos, arruinaremos todo el rompecabezas. Cuando la naturaleza está equilibrada, las plantas y los animales se mantienen felices, ¡y nosotros también!

Por eso es importante proteger a todos los animales, especialmente a los grandes. ¡Ayudan a que el mundo funcione correctamente!

El fin.

El lobo: un animal especial

Hace mucho tiempo, a la gente no le gustaban mucho los lobos. En muchas historias, a los lobos se les llamaba con nombres malos y se pensaba que daban miedo. En una historia de un lugar llamado Noruega, ¡un lobo llamado Fenrir fue llamado monstruo! En otros lugares, la gente pensaba que los lobos eran astutos o incluso malos disfrazados.

¿Has oído la historia del "Lobo feroz"? Es sólo una historia, pero hizo que mucha gente pensara que los lobos daban miedo. Incluso hoy en día, algunas personas siguen pensando que los lobos son animales malos. ¿Pero adivina qué? ¡Los lobos no dan tanto miedo como los hacen parecer las historias!

Los lobos no son tan malos

Los lobos cazan para encontrar comida, al igual que lo hacen los osos y los zorros. A veces, los lobos pueden comer animales de granja, pero no quieren lastimar a las personas. Es muy raro que los lobos lastimen a los humanos. Entonces, ¿por qué la gente piensa que los lobos son malos? Quizás sea por todas esas historias, pero en la vida real los lobos son animales muy especiales.

Algunas personas incluso usan la palabra "lobo" de maneras divertidas que no tienen sentido. ¿Alguna vez has oído a alguien silbar cuando ve algo que le gusta? Eso se llama "silbido de lobo", ¡pero los lobos no actúan así en absoluto! En realidad, los lobos son muy leales. Se quedan con la misma pareja de por vida, ¡lo cual es mejor que algunas personas!

Los lobos aman a sus familias

Los lobos viven en grupos llamados manadas. Sólo la mamá y el papá lobo de la manada tienen bebés, llamados cachorros. La madre loba caza con la manada y trae comida para sus cachorros. Los lobos se cuidan unos a otros e incluso protegerán a su familia del peligro. A veces, un lobo será tan valiente que arriesgará su vida para mantener a su familia a salvo.

Hay una historia famosa de hace mucho tiempo sobre dos hermanos llamados Rómulo y Remo. ¡Fueron criados por lobos y luego se convirtieron en los fundadores de la ciudad de Roma! Debido a esta historia, el lobo sigue siendo hoy el animal nacional de Italia.

Los lobos son súper inteligentes

Los lobos son muy inteligentes y trabajan en equipo. Cuando cazan juntos, pueden capturar animales más grandes que ellos, ¡como los alces! Por eso el equipo deportivo de la Universidad de Nevada se llama "Manada de lobos", porque los lobos son leales, inteligentes y valientes.

Los lobos y los perros son familia

¿Sabías que los lobos están estrechamente relacionados con los perros? ¡Incluso los perros pequeños, como los chihuahuas, están relacionados con los lobos! Hace mucho tiempo, los lobos de un lugar llamado Israel transmitieron su pequeño tamaño especial a los perros pequeños. Es un misterio cómo estos pequeños perros llegaron a lugares como Guatemala, pero podrían haber sido marineros que los trajeron a través del océano en sus barcos.

Los lobos son importantes

Los lobos son cariñosos, fuertes y leales. Son los primos salvajes de los perros que amamos hoy. Lamentablemente ya no hay tantos lobos como antes. Alguna vez hubo más de 2 millones de lobos, pero ahora solo quedan unos 200.000 en estado salvaje.

Los lobos no son las criaturas "grandes y malas" de los cuentos de hadas. ¡Son animales importantes y debemos ayudar a protegerlos!

El fin.

El asombroso ornitorrinco con pico de pato

¡El ornitorrinco es un animal genial de Australia! Es realmente especial porque es un mamífero, pero pone huevos como un pájaro. ¡Descubramos más sobre esta increíble criatura!

¿Qué aspecto tiene?

¡El ornitorrinco parece estar hecho de partes de diferentes animales! Tiene un pelaje grueso para mantenerse caliente en el agua, y la parte superior de su pelaje es marrón mientras que su vientre es más claro. Tiene una cola plana como la del castor, que le ayuda a nadar y almacenar comida. ¡Un ornitorrinco adulto mide casi tanto como un gato!

Pero lo más divertido del ornitorrinco es su pico grande y suave, ¡que parece el de un pato! Utiliza el pico para encontrar comida bajo el agua sintiendo pequeños movimientos. ¡El ornitorrinco puede incluso usar su pico para cavar una madriguera en la que vivir!

Un gran nadador

¡Al ornitorrinco le encanta nadar! Tiene patas palmeadas que le ayudan a moverse fácilmente en los ríos. Es tan bueno nadando que puede cerrar los ojos, los oídos y la nariz para evitar que entre el agua. El ornitorrinco está principalmente activo durante la noche, pero a veces también nada durante el día. Le gusta estar solo y mantiene a otros animales alejados de su espacio.

¿Qué come?

Aunque el ornitorrinco se ve lindo, ¡come carne! Pero no te preocupes: sólo come criaturas diminutas como insectos, gusanos y cangrejos. El ornitorrinco se sumerge bajo el agua para buscar comida con su pico. Recoge barro y escupe la tierra, manteniendo la comida en la boca. ¡A veces incluso guarda comida en sus mejillas!

Salvando al ornitorrinco

Lamentablemente, ya no hay tantos ornitorrincos como antes porque sus hogares están siendo destruidos y el agua se está ensuciando.

Pero la gente está tratando de ayudar protegiendo sus hogares y manteniendo el agua limpia.

El ornitorrinco es un animal asombroso con rasgos de diferentes tipos de criaturas, ¡lo que lo convierte en uno de los animales más geniales de la naturaleza! ¡Podemos ayudar a proteger al ornitorrinco para que pueda vivir por mucho, mucho tiempo!

La maravillosa mariposa monarca

La mariposa monarca es un hermoso insecto con alas de color naranja brillante y negro. ¡Puedes encontrarlos en lugares como América del Norte, México e incluso partes de América del Sur! Las monarcas son súper especiales y nos recuerdan lo maravillosa que es la naturaleza.

vida de un monarca

La vida de una mariposa monarca comienza como un pequeño huevo en una hoja de algodoncillo. Cuando el huevo eclosiona, sale una oruga bebé, llamada larva. A estas orugas les encanta comer una sola cosa: ¡algodoncillo!

Después de comer y crecer, la oruga forma un caparazón especial llamado crisálida. ¡Dentro de la crisálida sucede algo mágico! La oruga se transforma en mariposa en un proceso llamado metamorfosis. Una vez que la mariposa está lista, sale de la crisálida y se va volando.

Un viaje como ningún otro

Las mariposas monarca son famosas por sus largos viajes, llamados migración. Cuando el clima se vuelve más frío, vuelan a lugares más cálidos en el sur, como México, ¡viajando miles de millas! Cuando llega la primavera, vuelan de regreso al punto de partida. ¡Este largo viaje es una de las cosas más geniales de la naturaleza!

Salvando a los Reyes

Las mariposas monarca están en peligro porque sus hogares están siendo destruidos y las plantas de algodoncillo están desapareciendo. ¡Pero la gente está ayudando! Los grupos están trabajando arduamente para proteger a las mariposas monarca y sus hogares para que puedan quedarse con nosotros.

La mariposa monarca nos muestra lo maravillosa que es la naturaleza y por qué es importante cuidar nuestro planeta. ¡Ayudemos a proteger estas increíbles mariposas!

¡Salva al rinoceronte blanco!

El rinoceronte, o rinoceronte para abreviar, es uno de los animales más grandes de la Tierra; ¡solo los elefantes son más grandes! Hay dos tipos de rinocerontes: el rinoceronte negro y el rinoceronte blanco. El rinoceronte blanco tiene dos tipos, llamados rinoceronte blanco del norte y rinoceronte blanco del sur.

¿Por qué están desapareciendo los rinocerontes?

Los rinocerontes están en problemas por culpa de la gente. Algunas personas los cazan por sus cuernos, que pueden venderse por mucho dinero: ¡hasta 400.000 dólares! ¡Eso es incluso más que oro! Debido a que se cazan tantos rinocerontes, les resulta difícil mantenerse con vida. En este momento, sólo quedan dos rinocerontes blancos del norte en todo el mundo, ¡y ambas son niñas!

¿Podemos salvar a los rinocerontes?

¡Pero no te preocupes, todavía hay esperanza! Antes de que falleciera el último rinoceronte blanco del norte, los científicos salvaron sus células especiales y las congelaron. ¡Esto significa que algún día podrían ayudar a crear crías de rinoceronte!

Sin embargo, hay otro problema. Puede que no queden óvulos sanos de las niñas rinoceronte para formar nuevas crías de rinoceronte. Los científicos están tratando de solucionar este problema utilizando algo llamado células madre, que son células especiales que pueden convertirse en diferentes tipos de células, como las que producen óvulos.

Las células madre también pueden ayudar a los científicos a encontrar curas para enfermedades e incluso podrían ayudar a las personas a caminar nuevamente.

La gran pregunta

Si bien los científicos hacen cosas maravillosas, algunas personas se preocupan por cómo se recolectan las células madre. Provienen de bebés diminutos llamados embriones, y algunos grupos no están de acuerdo con eso. Es una gran discusión sobre lo que está bien y lo que está mal.

¡Pero ahora mismo podemos ayudar! Quizás no podamos recuperar animales como los mamuts lanudos, ¡pero podemos evitar que la gente cace rinocerontes y proteger a los que tenemos!

¡Trabajemos todos juntos para salvar a los rinocerontes antes de que sea demasiado tarde!

¡El misterio de la tortuga!

Érase una vez la gente pensaba que todos los científicos estaban de acuerdo en todo. ¿Pero adivina qué? ¡Eso no es cierto en absoluto! Los científicos suelen tener ideas diferentes, especialmente sobre los animales. ¡Y un gran misterio hoy tiene que ver con las tortugas!

¿Cómo pensaban los científicos?

Durante mucho tiempo, los científicos llamados biólogos (así llamamos a los científicos que estudian los seres vivos) agruparon a los animales según su apariencia. Entonces, los animales que parecían similares, como tortugas y lagartos, fueron puestos en el mismo grupo. La mayoría de los científicos pensaban que las tortugas eran parientes cercanos de las serpientes y los lagartos.

¡Una nueva idea!

¡Entonces sucedió algo increíble! Nuevos científicos llamados biólogos moleculares comenzaron a observar a los animales de una manera diferente. En lugar de simplemente observar el aspecto de los animales, estudiaron pequeños bloques de construcción dentro de seres vivos llamados proteínas. Pensaban que los animales con proteínas similares estaban más estrechamente relacionados, ¡aunque no se parecieran!

La sorpresa de la tortuga

En 2012, una científica llamada Ylenia Chiari tuvo una idea sorprendente. Se preguntó si las tortugas podrían parecerse más a los pájaros que a las serpientes o los lagartos. ¿Puedes creerlo? Tortugas y pájaros, ¡mejores amigos!

Para averiguarlo, un grupo de científicos estudió una proteína especial en la sangre de una tortuga de Galápagos, que es una de las tortugas más grandes del mundo. Compararon la proteína de la tortuga con la de otros animales utilizando una computadora súper inteligente. ¡Era como un juego de combinación de animales!

Esto es lo que encontraron:

- Por supuesto, la proteína de la tortuga de Galápagos coincidía estrechamente con la de otras tortugas.

- ¿Pero el siguiente en la fila? ¡A los pájaros les gustan los patos, los pingüinos y las gallinas! ¡Así es, gallinas!

- Incluso descubrieron que las tortugas comparten algunas proteínas con los elefantes y... ¡personas como tú y como yo!

¿Qué quiere decir esto?

Los resultados fueron bastante claros: las tortugas están más estrechamente relacionadas con las aves que con los lagartos cuando observamos sus proteínas. ¡Es casi como si el árbol genealógico secreto de la tortuga se remontara a las aves, no a los reptiles!

Y aquí hay algo más en lo que pensar: si los humanos, las tortugas, las aves e incluso los elefantes comparten algunas de las mismas proteínas, ¿no significa eso que todas las criaturas vivientes están conectadas? Quizás esa sea una gran razón para que tratemos a todos los animales con amabilidad y respeto.

El mundo de la ciencia está lleno de misterios y, a veces, ¡las respuestas son incluso más sorprendentes de lo que pensamos!

¡Salva al manatí!

¡Conoce al manatí, un gentil gigante del mar! Estas asombrosas criaturas son grandes y lentas, y les encanta nadar en aguas costeras cálidas. Al igual que nosotros, los manatíes son mamíferos, lo que significa que respiran aire y cuidan a sus crías.

¿Qué comen los manatíes?

Los manatíes adultos pueden pesar entre 1200 y 1500 libras, ¡guau! ¡Es como tener un coche pequeño nadando en el océano! Cada día, mastican hasta 150 libras de plantas, principalmente pastos marinos que crecen en el fondo del océano. ¡Les encanta tanto comer estas sabrosas verduras que hace mucho tiempo los marineros podrían haberlas confundido con sirenas!

Protegiendo a nuestros gentiles gigantes

Aunque los manatíes no tienen depredadores naturales, todavía necesitan nuestra ayuda. Existe una ley especial llamada Ley de Protección de Mamíferos Marinos que hace ilegal dañarlos. Se podría pensar que sin depredadores y con mucha comida, habría muchos manatíes, pero lamentablemente eso no es cierto. En 2021, más de 1.100 manatíes murieron, en su mayoría por inanición provocada por la contaminación.

Manatíes en Florida

La mayoría de los manatíes se pueden encontrar en las cálidas lagunas de Florida. Una laguna es un tipo especial de agua separada del océano por arena o coral. Estas aguas tranquilas son ideales para nadar, pero también atraen a muchos barcos y pescadores, lo que puede resultar peligroso para nuestros amigos que se mueven lentamente.

Los manatíes no son muy rápidos y sólo tienen seis huesos en el cuello en lugar de los siete que tienen la mayoría de los mamíferos. ¡Esto les dificulta girar la cabeza y mirar a su alrededor! Salen a tomar aire cada cinco minutos, pero a veces aparecen accidentalmente justo delante de lanchas rápidas y motos acuáticas. Muchos manatíes resultan heridos en accidentes o quedan atrapados en redes de pesca.

El verdadero peligro: el hambre

El mayor problema para los manatíes es en realidad el hambre. Florida es un lugar hermoso donde muchas plantas crecen bien gracias a los fertilizantes que la gente usa en sus jardines. Pero cuando llueve, estos químicos llegan a las lagunas y hacen que las algas dañinas crezcan demasiado. Esto se llama floración de algas.

Normalmente, los manatíes comerían pastos marinos, pero estas floraciones de algas impiden que la luz del sol llegue a las plantas de abajo, provocando la muerte de los pastos marinos. Sin su comida favorita, los manatíes pasan hambre y se debilitan.

¡Cómo puedes ayudar!

Si queremos salvar a los manatíes, ¡tenemos que actuar! El Departamento de Pesca y Vida Silvestre de los Estados Unidos y el Estado de Florida están trabajando juntos para solucionar los problemas de contaminación. ¡Tres grupos ambientalistas incluso están tomando medidas para proteger los hogares de los manatíes!

Si quieres ayudar, puedes apoyar a estas organizaciones:

- **Centro para la Diversidad Biológica**
378 calle principal
Tucson, AZ 85701
- **Defensores de la vida silvestre**
1130 calle 17 noroeste
Washington, DC 20036
- **Salva el club de manatíes**
533 Versailles Dr., Ste 100
Maitland, Florida 32751

¡Unámonos para salvar a los manatíes y mantener limpios nuestros océanos! Recuerde, ¡es importante cuidar nuestro planeta y todas sus criaturas, grandes y pequeñas!

La leyenda de Bigfoot: un misterio divertido

¿Alguna vez has oído hablar de Pie Grande? ¡Bigfoot es una criatura grande y peluda sobre la que la gente ha estado contando historias durante mucho tiempo! Algunas personas piensan que Bigfoot es real y otras no. Pero ¿por qué tanta gente sigue hablando de esta criatura gigante?

Una historia realmente antigua

¡La historia de Bigfoot es súper antigua! Hace más de 1.000 años, un hombre llamado Leif Erikson llegó a Estados Unidos y dijo que vio a un hombre gigante y peludo en el bosque. ¿Y adivina qué? Los nativos americanos de California también contaban historias sobre un hombre grande y peludo, e incluso lo dibujaban en las rocas. ¿No es genial?

La gente todavía ve Pie Grande

¡Incluso hoy la gente dice que ve Pie Grande! En 2022, alguien en Carolina del Sur dijo que vio una criatura grande y peluda en un parque. ¡Un hombre llamado Dennis encontró huellas gigantes que se parecían a otras huellas encontradas en montañas lejanas! La gente ha estado viendo Bigfoot durante mucho tiempo, en todo el país.

Un gran libro sobre Bigfoot

¿Sabías que el gobierno incluso escribió sobre Bigfoot? En 1975, un libro sobre la naturaleza en el estado de Washington hablaba de Bigfoot o Sasquatch. ¡Dijeron que Bigfoot podía medir entre 8 y 12 pies de alto y pesar tanto como un automóvil pequeño! La gente dice que Bigfoot tiene pelo largo y pies grandes, y que podría comer plantas y algo de carne.

El misterio del Pie Grande

Bigfoot es muy tímido y no deja muchas pistas. A veces, la gente encuentra huellas gigantes e incluso hay una película corta de una criatura que podría ser Pie Grande. Algunas personas piensan que la película es falsa, pero otros creen que es real.

Entonces, ¿qué opinas? ¿Bigfoot es real o es sólo una historia divertida? No lo sabemos con certeza, ¡y eso es lo que lo convierte en un gran misterio! ¡Mantén tu mente abierta y diviértete explorando lo desconocido!

El misterio del chihuahua y los marineros

¿Alguna vez has visto un pequeño chihuahua y pensaste que parecía un lobo? ¡Es cierto! Los chihuahuas, como todos los perros, están relacionados con los lobos. Los científicos estudian los genes de los perros para aprender más sobre el origen de los diferentes perros. Pero, ¿cómo se hizo tan pequeño el pequeño chihuahua?

El secreto de sus genes

¿Sabías que todos los perros, incluso los grandes como el gran danés, comparten casi el mismo ADN? ¡Hay un gen especial en los perros pequeños que los mantiene pequeños y se llama IGF-1! Este gen les dice a sus cuerpos que permanezcan pequeños, por lo que los chihuahuas no crecen tanto como otros perros.

Pero ¿por qué los chihuahuas se volvieron tan pequeños? Hace mucho tiempo, personas como los mayas criaron lobos para hacer perros más pequeños. Otra idea es que cuando los españoles llegaron a América, sus perros se mezclaron con los perros locales. Y luego está la idea del Marinero Antiguo: ¡hablemos de eso!

La antigua idea del marinero

Algunas personas piensan que marineros venidos de lugares lejanos, tal vez cercanos a Israel, llegaron a México hace mucho, mucho tiempo: ¡alrededor del año 600 a.C.! Es posible que estos marineros hubieran traído consigo a sus perros pequeños. Esos perros podrían haberse mezclado con los perros de México y, con el tiempo, se convirtieron en los chihuahuas que conocemos hoy.

Otros perros pequeños con secretos

Los chihuahuas no son los únicos perros pequeños con genes especiales. Hay otros perros, como el Sin Pelo Mexicano y el Crestado Chino, que no tienen mucho pelo. Todos comparten un gen especial que los deja sin pelo. ¿Cómo llegaron estos perros sin pelo a diferentes países? ¡Quizás los antiguos marineros los llevaban en sus largos viajes!

Un largo viaje sobre el mar

Si esos antiguos marineros realmente lo visitaron, podría ayudar a explicar cómo surgieron los perros diminutos como los chihuahuas. ¡La gente incluso ha encontrado obras de arte antiguas que muestran perros pequeños de hace mucho tiempo! Quizás los marineros compartían sus perros cuando visitaban nuevos lugares y llevaban a estos pequeños amigos al otro lado del mar.

¿Cuál es la mejor explicación?

Hay muchas ideas sobre el origen de los chihuahuas, pero a veces la respuesta más sencilla es la mejor. ¿Podría ser que los antiguos marineros trajeran a sus perritos a través del océano, ayudando a crear el chihuahua que vemos hoy? La ciencia aún no ha resuelto el misterio, pero una cosa es segura: ¡cada chihuahua tiene una gran historia!

About the Author

Dr. Robert H. Stauffer Jr. is a renowned physics educator, author, and columnist. He has written numerous books, including The World Chess Champions. Driven by his passion for the game, Dr. Stauffer authored this book to share his love of chess with players of all ages and skill levels, helping them improve their understanding and enjoyment of the game.

www.ingramcontent.com/pod-product-compliance
Lightning Source LLC
Chambersburg PA
CBHW051316160726
47994CB00003B/1480